ON THE
WORLD STAGE

SPOTLIGHT ON

Nigeria

Ngeri Nnachi-Azuewah

Lerner Publications ◆ Minneapolis

Content consultant: Dr. Abdulai Iddrisu, Director, Africa and the African Diaspora Program, St. Olaf College

Lerner Publications Company
An imprint of Lerner Publishing Group, Inc.
241 First Avenue North
Minneapolis, MN 55401 USA

For reading levels and more information, look up this title at www.lernerbooks.com.

Main body text set in Aptifer Sans LT Pro Semibold.
Typeface provided by Linotype AG.

Designer: Athena Currier

Library of Congress Cataloging-in-Publication Data

Names: Nnachi, Ngeri, author.
Title: Spotlight on Nigeria / Ngeri Nnachi-Azuewah.
Description: Minneapolis : Lerner Publications, [2024] | Series: Countries on the world
    stage | Includes bibliographical references and index. | Audience: Ages 8–12 | Audience:
    Grades 4–6 | Summary: "With the largest population in Africa, Nigeria is an economic
    powerhouse. Uncover Nigeria's history, learn how it became a global power in energy
    and entertainment, and see what's in store for the future of the country"— Provided by
    publisher.
Identifiers: LCCN 2022043013 (print) | LCCN 2022043014 (ebook) | ISBN 9781728492018 (lib.
    bdg.) | ISBN 9798765602577 (paperback) | ISBN 9781728496665 (eb pdf)
Subjects: LCSH: Nigeria—Juvenile literature.
Classification: LCC DT515.22 .N58 2024 (print) | LCC DT515.22 (ebook) | DDC 966.9—dc23/
    eng/20220923

LC record available at https://lccn.loc.gov/2022043013
LC ebook record available at https://lccn.loc.gov/2022043014

Manufactured in the United States of America
1-53140-51150-1/5/2023

TABLE OF CONTENTS

INTRODUCTION

Independence Day

OCTOBER 1, 1960, WAS A NIGHT THAT MANY WOULD NEVER FORGET. Thousands gathered at a large sports field in Lagos. Princess Alexandra attended the event, representing her cousin, Queen Elizabeth II of Britain. Nigerian prime minister Sir Abubakar Tafawa Balewa was also at the event. He had worked hard for many years for this moment. Just before midnight, the lights went out. In the darkness, the British Union Jack flag was lowered. Then, as the clock struck midnight, the lights were switched back on, and the

Nigerian Interdependence Day is celebrated with parades and fireworks.

green-and-white flag of Nigeria flew above the crowds. It was the end of the fight for Nigerian independence, but it was just the beginning of the story for the new Nigeria.

CHAPTER 1

Nigeria through the Ages

Archaeologists have found evidence that humans have lived in Nigeria since at least 9000 BCE, but the first society we have evidence of is the Nok culture. The Nok culture started around 500 BCE and ended around 200 CE. The people created sculptures out of terra-cotta and tools out of iron.

The Igbo Kingdom of Nri, which appeared on the southern coast around the tenth century, created some of the oldest bronze statues in the region. In the north, the Hausa states

Artists in the Kingdom of Benin created sculptures in bronze, ivory, and wood.

rose around the fourteenth century and traded with people from across the Sahara.

In 1440 the Edo people founded the Kingdom of Benin in what is now southwest Nigeria. The Kingdom of Benin was not related to the modern-day country of Benin. This kingdom traded with the Portuguese, who sought its artwork, gold, ivory, and pepper. The Kingdom of Benin was strongest from the 1200s to the 1800s. The Kingdom of Benin started losing its power in the 1800s when royal family members began to fight for control of the throne. By 1897 the Kingdom of Benin was taken over by the British.

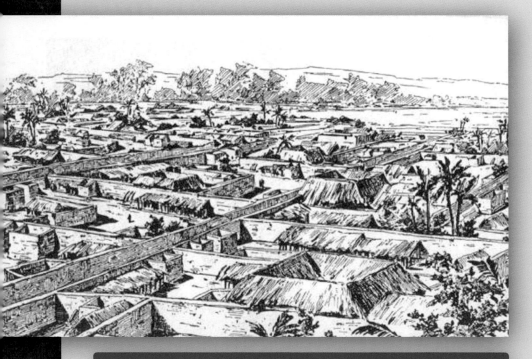

Benin City, the capital of the Kingdom of Benin, was destroyed by the British in 1897.

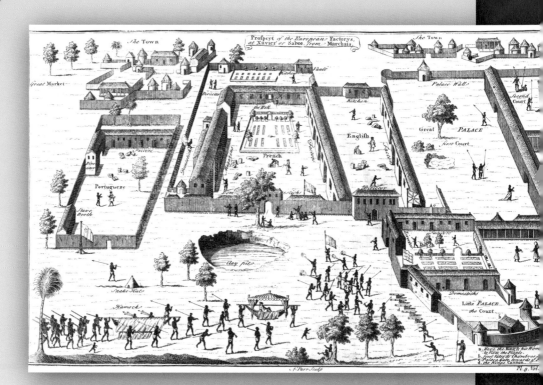

Prospect of the European Factorys, at Xavier or Sabee, from Marchais.

European traders captured and imprisoned African people in compounds on the Gulf of Guinea before enslaving them.

   In 1884, during the Berlin Conference, European leaders gathered to discuss how they would divide and colonize Africa. During this meeting, they started reorganizing the boundaries of African ethnic groups, assembling different peoples into new countries that European governments could control. The country of Nigeria was created in 1914 by combining two regions controlled by the United Kingdom, the Northern and the Southern Nigeria Protectorates.

As far back as 1947, Nigeria began sending delegations to the United Kingdom to demand independence. Among these delegations were Nnamdi Azikiwe, the first president of Nigeria, and Prime Minister Balewa. It took many decades, but Nigeria finally became an independent country on October 1, 1960.

However, not everyone agreed about how to run this new country. A group of Igbo people in the south felt the government was not listening to them. They declared independence from Nigeria and formed the Republic of Biafra in 1967, starting the Nigerian Civil War that ended in 1970.

The Nigerian army attacked the newly independent Republic of Biafra on July 6, 1967.

NIGERIA'S NATIONAL YOUTH SERVICE CORPS

After the Nigerian Civil War, the government created the National Youth Service Corps to encourage young people to engage in civil service and develop national unity. As of 1973, university graduates have been required to serve one year in the National Youth Service Corps. Corps members are sent to different regions to connect with people from across Nigeria.

CHAPTER 2

Land and People

Nigeria is in western Africa, with Benin to the west, Cameroon to the east, and Niger and Chad to the north. It borders the Atlantic Ocean to the south and has three climate zones: a tropical monsoon climate in its southern region, a tropical savanna climate for most of its central regions, and a Sahelian hot and semiarid climate in its northern region. It has a distinct rainy season with the heaviest rainfalls happening between May and October.

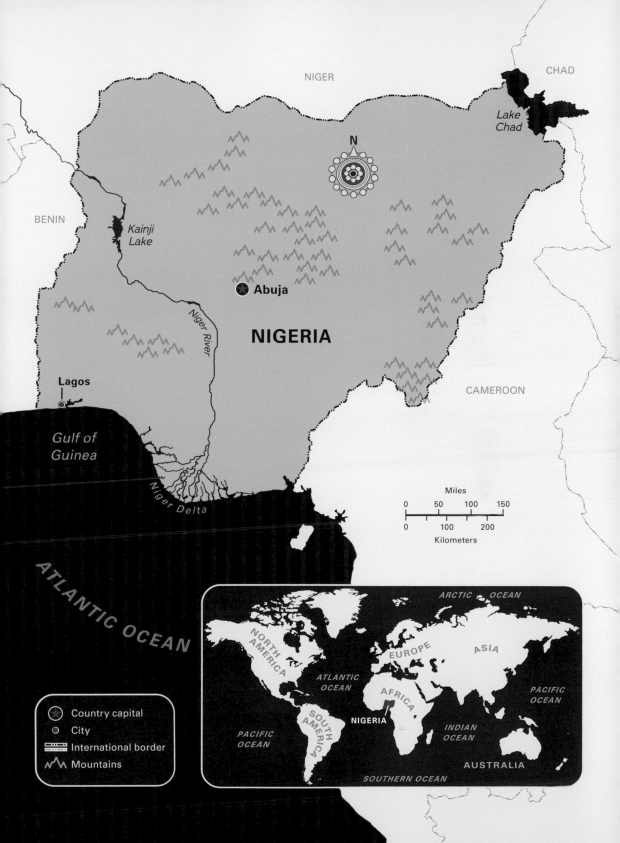

NIGER

CHAD

Lake
Chad

N

BENIN

Kainji
Lake

Abuja

NIGERIA

Niger River

CAMEROON

Lagos

Gulf of
Guinea

Niger Delta

Miles
| 0 | 50 | 100 | 150 |

| 0 | 100 | 200 |

Kilometers

ATLANTIC OCEAN

ARCTIC OCEAN

NORTH AMERICA

EUROPE

ASIA

ATLANTIC OCEAN

AFRICA

PACIFIC OCEAN

PACIFIC OCEAN

SOUTH AMERICA

NIGERIA

INDIAN OCEAN

AUSTRALIA

SOUTHERN OCEAN

Country capital
City
International border
Mountains

Nigeria has a variety of terrains including deserts, swamps, plains, and mountains. The country is home to one of the largest river deltas in the world, the Niger delta.

Nigeria is made up of thirty-six states and is home to over two hundred million people. Its largest city is Lagos. It was the capital city until December 1991, when Abuja became the capital. But Lagos remains Nigeria's leading commercial and industrial city.

There are over 371 ethnic groups that call Nigeria home. The top three groups are the Hausa in the north and the Igbo and the Yoruba in the south. Ethnic tensions are frequent, leading to many conflicts throughout the country.

The rainy season in Nigeria can last from March until November.

NIGERIAN AUTHORS

Chinua Achebe was a world-renowned poet and novelist who wrote the famous 1958 book *Things Fall Apart*. This book has sold more than twenty million copies and has been translated into more than fifty languages. Another popular Nigerian writer is Chimamanda Ngozi Adichie, who is most known for writing about the Nigerian Civil War in her novel *Half of a Yellow Sun*.

Over five hundred languages are spoken in the country. The official language is English. Many Nigerians speak Nigerian pidgin, which is a simplified form of English that is easier to learn and helps people talk to one another across the country. Different ethnic groups have their own languages, and within some languages there can be many ways of speaking those languages. These are called dialects. For example, the Igbo language has approximately thirty dialects.

CHAPTER 3

A Changing Economy

Oil was discovered in the Niger delta in 1956. Nigeria is currently the world's thirteenth-largest producer of crude oil. The money from this boom was used to grow the transportation, construction, and manufacturing industries, and it brought more people into urban areas.

The oil palm tree is native to Nigeria, making palm oil an important product for the country.

Researchers in Nigeria are creating new types of oil palm trees that are smaller and easier to grow.

Urban migration meant that there were fewer people to grow crops. Nigeria had to start importing foods such as rice and cassava for people who relied on these staples. These changes, as well as political instability and soil damage due to climate change, have created a food crisis that is still being felt. But more than a third of Nigeria's workforce still work in agriculture. In rural areas, many farmers grow yams, cassava, rice, and corn. Some farmers grow cash crops such as palm oil and peanuts.

Nigeria has been innovative in its approach to the country's economy. The Central Bank of Nigeria created the eNaira in 2021, a digital form of the Nigerian currency, the naira. It was created to make it easier for Nigerians to access money on a smartphone and pay for things.

Nigeria's entertainment industry has grown in recent years. Nollywood, which stands for "Nigerian Hollywood," is a huge part of Nigeria's economy and has worked with companies such as Netflix and YouTube. Nigerian movies have become more popular around the world.

The Millennium Tower and Cultural Centre is the tallest structure in Abuja, Nigeria.

CHAPTER 4

Democracy in Nigeria

Nigeria gained independence from the United Kingdom on October 1, 1960. After that it became a British Commonwealth for three years. At the time, Nigeria had a president and a prime minister. Nigeria declared Azikiwe its first president and Balewa its first and only prime minister upon independence. Both served until the government was overthrown in a military coup in 1966. A military government ruled Nigeria until 1979, when Nigeria elected Shehu Shagari as its

The National Assembly of Nigeria meets in the capital city of Abuja, Nigeria.

president, making him the second elected president of Nigeria. Shagari served until 1983.

A VISIT FROM MARTIN LUTHER KING JR.

Azikiwe wrote a letter to Martin Luther King Jr., inviting him to Lagos to attend his inauguration. King accepted the invitation. The American civil rights leader was inspired by the liberation movement in Africa, saying it offered young people in the US hope in their own fight for civil rights.

Nnamdi Azikiwe, Nigeria's first president

Nigeria was again ruled by a military government from 1983 until 1999, when President Olusegun Obasanjo was elected. He was the third president elected by the people. Obasanjo set out to tackle poverty and government corruption while establishing a democratic governing system. In 2015 Nigeria elected Muhammadu Buhari president. He had previously led the country as a military head of state.

Under the 1999 Nigerian Constitution, Nigeria became a federal republic again. The president and members of the National Assembly, who write Nigeria's laws, are elected by popular vote every four years. Voters in each of Nigeria's thirty-six states elect ten representatives and three senators to the National Assembly. In 2006 an amendment was voted on by the National Assembly to remove the two-term limit for the president, meaning one person could be elected president more than two times. But this amendment was voted down.

The president of Nigeria has the power to sign a bill or veto it, stopping it from becoming law unless the National Assembly has enough votes to override the veto.

Nigeria in the Twenty-First Century

Nigerians are hopeful for the future.
The entertainment, communications, and technology
industries are growing and making Nigeria a global power.
But Nigeria faces many challenges. The country imports
a lot of its food, which raises food prices. In 2019 Nigeria
closed its land borders to stop the smuggling of goods such
as rice and encouraged local farmers to grow more food
for the country. But attacks from armed bandits and soil

Droughts caused by climate change have made cattle ranching more difficult in Nigeria.

damage from climate change have forced many farmers to flee to cities where jobs can be hard to find. In 2019 the Nigerian government started the National Livestock Transformation Plan to boost food production and protect ranchers and farmers.

GREEN ENERGY

Even though it exports lots of oil, Nigeria struggles with energy shortages. The country has also been hit by extreme heat waves due to climate change, which cause people to use even more energy to run air-conditioning. In 2020 the Nigerian government ended subsidies for fossil fuel companies to encourage people to build more reliable green energy sources such as wind turbines and solar farms.

Solar energy is clean and renewable.

The naira, Nigeria's national currency, was introduced in 1973.

People are seeing what Nigeria has to offer through music videos and Netflix movies, which boosts their desire to visit the country. With tourism on the rise, Nigeria's economy will likely grow even more. The future of Nigeria is bright, promising reliable green energy, food security, and safer roads to travel.

TIMELINE

500 BCE–200 CE The Nok culture existed in central Nigeria.

1440–1897 The Kingdom of Benin controls southwest Nigeria.

1897 The British Empire takes control of the Kingdom of Benin.

1914 The United Kingdom establishes Nigeria as a protectorate.

1960 Nigeria gains independence from the British Empire.

1963 The Federal Republic of Nigeria is established.

1966 The Federal Military Government of Nigeria is formed.

1967 The Nigerian Civil War, or the Biafran War, starts.

1970 The Nigerian Civil War ends.

2006 The National Assembly of Nigeria votes against a constitutional amendment to remove the presidential term limit.

2020 The Nigerian government ends subsidies for fossil fuel companies to encourage a transition to green energy.

NIGERIA FAST FACTS

Name: Federal Republic of Nigeria

Population: 225,082,083

Land area: 356,669 square miles (923,768 sq. km)

Largest city: Lagos, population 15.388 million

Capital city: Abuja, population 3.652 million

Form of government: federal republic

Official language: English

Flag:

GLOSSARY

amendment: a change in wording or meaning, especially in a law, bill, or motion

archaeologist: one who studies material remains of past human life and activities

cash crop: a readily salable crop produced or gathered primarily for market

coup: a sudden exercise of force in politics and especially the violent overthrow or change of an existing government by a small group

delegation: one or more persons chosen to represent others

delta: a piece of land in the shape of a triangle or fan made by deposits of mud and sand at the mouth of a river

inauguration: act or ceremony of introducing a person into office

innovative: characterized by or introducing a new idea, method, or device

protectorate: the relationship of authority assumed by one power or state over a dependent one

subsidy: a grant by a government to a private person or company for assistance

terra-cotta: a glazed or unglazed fired clay used especially for statuettes, vases, and architectural purposes

LEARN MORE

Britannica Kids: Nigeria
https://kids.britannica.com/kids/article/Nigeria/345758

Doeden, Matt. *Travel to Nigeria*. Minneapolis: Lerner Publications, 2023.

Globe Trottin' Kids: Nigeria
https://www.globetrottinkids.com/countries/nigeria/

Hudak, Heather C. *Pathways through Africa*. New York: Crabtree, 2019.

Kiddle: Nigeria Facts for kids
https://kids.kiddle.co/Nigeria

Kids World Travel Guide: Nigeria Facts
https://www.kids-world-travel-guide.com/nigeria-facts.html

Nanz, Rosie. *Explore Nigeria: 12 Key Facts*. Mankato, MN: 12 Story Library, 2019.

National Geographic Kids: Nigeria
https://kids.nationalgeographic.com/geography/countries/article/nigeria

INDEX

PHOTO ACKNOWLEDGMENTS

Image credits: Houston/Xinhua/Getty Images, p. 5; Matt Neale from UK/Wikipedia (CC BY-SA 2.0), p. 7; CPA Media Pte Ltd/Alamy Stock Photo, p. 8; Science History Images/Alamy Stock Photo, p. 9; Olukayode Jaiyeola/NurPhoto/Getty Images, p. 10; Express Newspapers/Getty Images, p. 11; Laura Westlund/Independent Picture Service, p. 13; Hemis/Alamy Stock Photo, p. 14; Jonathan Sherrill/Alamy Stock Photo, p. 15; PIUS UTOMI EKPEI/AFP/Getty Images, p. 17; Joshua Paul/Bloomberg/Getty Images, p. 18; Em Campos/Alamy Stock Photo, p. 19; AP Photo, p. 21; Bettmann Archive/Getty Images, p. 22; REUTERS/Alamy Stock Photo, p. 23; Fela Sanu/iStockphoto/Getty Images, p. 25; jia yu/Moment/Getty Images, p. 26; Damilola Onafuwa/Bloomberg/Getty Images, p. 27; HM Design/Shutterstock, p. 29.

Cover: Kehinde Temitope Odutayo/Shutterstock.